B. E. P. I. C.

Be Seen & Be Heard

ISBN: 978-1-66781-541-1

Contents

Dedication

I dedicate this book to my son, Joshua Benjamin;
my dear parents, Michael and Valentina;
and my siblings, Ilya, Eleanor, and Virginia.

Preface

The path to becoming a successful entrepreneur and a recognized expert was one of the toughest challenges I have ever endured. It made me realize that you need more than just a plan, a thought, or an idea. You have to take action. Succeeding requires setting goals and working consistently to achieve them. You must have the will and determination to rise after every fall and remember every learned lesson. My secret to success is to fail as often as possible so that you can succeed sooner. Just keep rowing the boat; G-D will steer.

As the author who changed my mindset, Napoleon Hill, once said, "strength and growth come only through continuous effort and struggle." I've garnered many achievements in my life. But I still commit to improving myself because there is always room for improvement. We win some, and we lose some. I have some personal mantras I live by that help me feel strong, capable, and at peace. I proved to myself that I could become the first female businesswoman in my family despite the odds. We grow when learning from mistakes and rejoice after accomplishing victories. Remember that nobody achieved success without first experiencing struggles and failures.

In this competitive mass media industry, it's easy to get lost and frustrated when you can't find your voice and stand out. I wrote this book because I used to be unknown and invisible. I began my journey as a real estate agent, then transitioned to life insurance. After some time, I went into fashion and became a stylist and owner of a styling concierge firm. Finally, after years of searching, I decided to follow my passion for storytelling and became a public relations expert and a digital storyteller. I transitioned between career paths and reinvented myself every time to reach my highest potential. I always wanted to become an expert in helping clients gain exposure and attention through storytelling. However, I lacked essential direction and no online presence; therefore, I became social proof with the proper media training, mentors, and coaches. By being vulnerable and authentic with my personal story, I have gained visibility and credibility. I had difficulty setting myself apart from others. Fortunately, with the help of resources that honed my public relations skills and knowledge, I discovered a world where personal branding holds massive value. I feel strongly motivated to write this book and share the wisdom I've acquired from my mentors and experiences.

The most important mentors and motivators in my life are my loving parents. My father, my hero, is a successful restaurateur who has been disrupting the hospitality industry since 1987. He is a man of honor and integrity who taught me how to face adversity, the art of moving forward, and how to be the captain of my life. My mother, a beautiful and courageous soul who is a former gynecologist, taught me to surround myself with people who have a library more extensive than their television. I am grateful to have supportive and understanding parents.

However, my parents didn't always believe in my abilities and that I'd make it as a businesswoman someday. I used their doubts as fuel to propel myself forward. It is not common in our community and culture for a woman to lead an independent life, become a successful businesswoman and CEO. I am thankful that my parents challenged my mindset. Because of that, I made history as the first-ever female entrepreneur, CEO, and author in my family. I founded my companies using my resources, tenacity, and persistence.

I started unheard of but became unforgettable. My story is proof that anything is possible as long as you're determined to achieve your lifelong desires. As a divorcée, single mom, and college dropout at twenty-one years old, I conquered the hardships that shaped me into the confident woman I am now. Once lost as an insurance and real estate agent, then as a cosmetologist, and, finally, a traveling celebrity stylist, I wasn't entirely sure of the path I'd taken. It felt unfulfilling and empty. Thanks to my spiritual journey and Napoleon Hill's book,

Think and Grow Rich, I found my direction and mission in life. I became a public relations maven and a media mogul by discovering my passion for storytelling, authority, connecting with women who have a burning desire to share their stories with the world, uncovering the secrets of successful people, and passing them on to those who seek it.

This realization led me to create my podcast, *What Makes a Woman*, where I interview C-level executives about building business empires from the ground up. I am humbled and grateful; I have had the chance to converse with remarkable individuals like Sharon Lechter, the co-author of *Rich Dad Poor Dad* and editor of Napoleon Hill's *Outwitting the Devil*. Other notable figures include Forbes Riley, Tomi Lahren, Patrick Bet-David, Yahya Bakkar, Brad Lea, Dave Kerpen, Andrea Catsimatidis, Joy Taylor, Rudy Rochman, and many more. In my WMW show, I unraveled their best-kept secrets on defeating adversity and becoming key players in various industries. Through this medium, I have reached many people and influenced them to start their own business, follow their passion, gain confidence to speak up, and land media opportunities.

Even though 2020 was the most challenging year with Covid-19, it was the best year for my business despite chaos and uncertainty. I had to pivot and took my whole company remote. The pandemic propelled my agency tenfold since everything went digital. I decided to stay relevant during the most catastrophic time of our lives by helping women laid off and who couldn't find a job. My company released a pandemic relief program where we hired two hundred young women who had a knack for media and needed a freelance position. I doubled down on making more connections online than ever before. My team reached out to online personalities, celebrities, professionals, and C-level executives to speak on my daily show to instill positivity and confidence in times of uncertainty. My podcast show went viral.

The world was shutting down and impacting many people negatively. The most challenging factor for me was when my family's restaurant, ZAVO in NYC, had to shut down as most restaurants were affected by the pandemic. It was there that I became known as the PR

Maven, who expanded her family's restaurant in the press and media. I considered our restaurant my second home; it was a place of excitement, allure, and elegance. It was, in fact, the site where I launched my podcast show, What Makes A Woman, with incredible and groundbreaking guests! Zavo will always be a household name.

But I realized that in a losing situation, there is still an opportunity to win. I knew I had to carry on despite the hardships. I started putting energy into my show and reinvented myself during this tragic time. I began writing this book since it was always my dream to become an author and share my wealth of wisdom as an expert in my niche.

One thing led to another until I finally conceptualized this book. I wanted to impart the lessons that molded my entrepreneurial spirit and power. I formulated the BEPIC program to help women gain their powerful voice, share their groundbreaking success stories, become disruptors and recognized experts. Women need to be seen and heard on a national and international scope. ***WOMEN SHOULD NO***

LONGER STAY INVISIBLE, AND WE ARE BECOMING EPIC IN A MALE-DOMINATED WORLD.

The five BEPIC pillars are the pathway to ultimate authority and the use of their powerful voice. With these tools, the success stories shared by the renowned personalities above can become yours!

My mission is to give voice to the voiceless and create opportunities for brands and companies to gain maximum exposure, visibility, and credibility through storytelling. I want to inspire the next generation of entrepreneurs who want to be recognized as experts in their niche and help them land media opportunities using their strong personal brand. As the founder and CEO of ZavoMedia Group PR Agency, I'm here to help your story easily stand out and effectively make positive exposure and visibility to brands. Also, as chief editor of *my business and lifestyle magazine*, I develop and strategize PR campaigns and place compelling stories of recognized experts in top-tier publications. My media and communications company excels in giving entrepreneurs and professionals a platform with maximum exposure and an avenue to be seen and heard nationally and internationally. My specialty is developing personal branding and strategic partnerships with brands. In turn, it helps those with powerful and unique voices make an impact on the world. Our doors are always open for coaching and mentorship.

Lastly, I wrote this book for all the professionals, entrepreneurs, and C-level executives who have the burning desire to become recognized experts and the number one authorities in their niche. I want to uplift fellow entrepreneurs and professionals who want to be unique and make a difference. Who knows, you might be the next guest on my show and share your version of success with others.

In the words of a PR expert, branding maven, thought leader, business influencer, female advocate, and most importantly, a mother to a teenage son and a Bernedoodle named Da Vinci, *you are your greatest asset*. You can become epic as long as you desire it. It's a matter of when and how prepared you are to embrace your power. If not now, then when?

Life is a marathon, not a sprint. Those brave enough for change are a step closer to success. Are you ready to become epic? Flip to the next page if you're in for the most significant transformation of your life!

Introduction

Have you ever wanted to be heard but didn't dare speak your mind because you feared judgment? Are there other times when something held you back, keeping you from getting what you wanted or doing what you always wanted to do? Like most people, feeling powerless, lost, and voiceless like this comes all too frequently.

But they don't have to.

Moments of weakness like the ones above keep us from achieving what we want. Why? Because we surrender to the word "can't." We limit ourselves to the belief that we can only do *this* and not *that*. The epic things we might accomplish will never happen if the negativity "can't" control us.

I wrote this book because I want you to unlock your potential to become an authority. I want to help you speak up, find your unique voice, and overcome those limiting beliefs that keep you from becoming the epic person you are.

I grew up in a Russian-Bukharian culture, where young girls like me have to become successful professionals like doctors and lawyers—but nothing grandiose like becoming an entrepreneur and a businesswoman (for men only!). I didn't have a voice under that pressure to succeed in predefined ways; I just did what society dictated. I had the burning desire to make my path, which became a guideline for other aspiring female businesswomen.

When I got married, I thought I could voice my opinions, become visible and an equal partner who makes decisions with her husband. Being married and having a child while going to college was the most demanding job I had to do. I believe in an equal partnership between a husband and wife while still embracing my femininity. Now some may call me a radical feminist, but I consider myself a lipstick feminist.

I knew my responsibilities as a Jewish wife, mother, college student, and working a part-time job would be intense, but I also thought I would have a supportive partner. I could handle only so much, and feeling alone, not heard, and invisible in my marriage was unacceptable. At age twenty, I decided it was best for my well-being to get a divorce and become my own woman.

Two years later, I dropped out of college since I couldn't follow my desired path. Public relations wasn't a popular degree to pursue in my community and because my parents talked me out of it. It was safe to study speech pathology since every girl did it from high school, but that was the most boring college journey I encountered. I was seeking excitement and not the traditional route. I was craving to be different, and I aspired to be a businesswoman on television and in the public eye. I had to play safe because I was a married woman and a mother in a conservative Jewish home. That type of traditional lifestyle I lived in, with no right to voice my opinion, stopped me from thriving and becoming an epic woman.

As hard as it was to leave, I decided to live an inspirational life for future generations and rise like a phoenix from the ashes. As Napoleon Hill shared: "Thousands of men and women carry inferiority complexes with them all through life, because some well-meaning, but ignorant person destroyed their confidence through 'opinions' or 'ridicule.'"

It's easy to point fingers. But in the end, I always had the power to make a choice, even if I didn't believe it at first. I realized that whatever path I took, there would be struggles and obstacles blocking the way. There's no point in blaming and making excuses because nothing happens because of it. It was up to me to decide whether I should remain silent or take action. I chose the latter.

In this journey called life, we pick the roads that lead us to our destination. It is our choices that bring us to the quality of life that we want. I had to find ways to overcome the restrictive structures I encountered.

I changed my mindset and opened my eyes to the countless possibilities that I could achieve in my life. It took me twenty years to break free from my limiting beliefs. That's how long I struggled to get to where I am today. But that's all on me. I had the power all along to realize that I was more than those fears and doubts, that I was more than those moments of hesitation and powerlessness.

You have that power too.

No matter who you are, where you're from, how old you are, or how much is in your bank account—you have the power to turn your life into an epic success. By following the five BEPIC pillars laid out in this book, you will have the tools to live a truly epic life:

- BELIEF—Turning Belief into Reality
- EMPOWERMENT—Speaking Your Power into Existence
- POWER—Gaining Power through Personal Satisfaction
- INNER VOICE—Finding Your Unique Voice & Speak Up
- COURAGE—Developing the Courage to Become the Number 1 Authority

You also have the power—the authority and influence—to pave your way to the successful future you're meant to have. All you have to do is tap into it!

Belief

Turning Belief into Reality

*

I know of no single formula for success. But over the years, I have observed that some attributes of leadership are universal and are often about finding ways of encouraging people to combine their efforts, their talents, their insights, their enthusiasm, and their inspiration to work together.

I have to be seen to be believed.

—Queen Elizabeth II, Monarch Reigning Over the United Kingdom and Fifteen Other Commonwealth realms

Turning a belief into reality is not so common, even though it should be part of our daily habits to become unstoppable. It also means putting trust in a person or a thing. What you perceive as acceptable in your eyes becomes your belief. Beliefs come from facts, opinions, or assumptions. They can also originate from your own experiences and interactions with your surroundings. As long as you believe in something, you tend to stick to it. More often than not, your beliefs influence what you do, say, and think.

When we hear the term "self-limiting beliefs," we think of negative perceptions rooted in past experiences, familial traditions, and even social media influence. While it's true that we grew up with rules and restrictions as children, relics of those rules can become limiting beliefs that prevent us from realizing our full potential.

If these limiting beliefs persist, they form into doubts. When doubts settle in, you end up not having complete confidence in yourself. It leads to a big load of anxiety and second-guessing that keeps you from performing your best and living life to the fullest. You question the validity of your life decisions and lose confidence in what you do.

I lacked belief in myself because of my upbringing. My failed marriage also added fuel to the fire. I never knew the power and capabilities I had because of the limiting beliefs and restrictive environment. Fortunately, I managed to move forward and cultivate the qualities that a leader and entrepreneur must possess through these steps.

First, you need to assess your behavior and outlook in life. Is there something that hinders you from doing your best? These are some of the signs indicating that you might have limiting beliefs:

- Feeling worthless and powerless and acting defensively
- Thinking everything should be perfect so you can avoid judgment
- Avoiding conflict by giving in to others
- Resisting change because of fear of the unknown
- Having that feeling of not being good enough

You must identify your self-limiting beliefs. List the negative thoughts that you often think about, and determine when they started. What made you doubtful and conflicted about yourself and the decisions you've made? Knowing where your limiting beliefs come from helps you understand how and why they formed. In my case, it was the culture and environment of my childhood that created barriers. I jumped from one career to another because it piqued my interest. I wanted to experience different areas of life and meet new and creative individuals. Learning a unique niche, meeting the right people at the right time, and becoming a well-rounded individual taught me to turn my belief into reality.

I had countless moments of self-sabotage, and those self-limiting beliefs got the best of me. One day, I decided to start writing my story on my terms as I always envisioned it. Until I met the right people who believed in me, I wasn't going in the right direction. It takes a village to help one to become a successful person. Looking back and connecting all the dots makes sense why other doors shut in my face. Hundreds of no's were leading me to my purpose. Sometimes it takes one person to change your life completely, and I was fortunate enough to have encountered a powerful woman. My introduction to this inspirational woman, Mirela Matan, helped turn my belief into reality. At that time, I was working at Bergdorf Goodman, styling clients as a freelancer. She approached me and asked to represent her skincare line because she saw something in me in my vision for her brand. I dealt only with fashion brands; however, my conversation sparked an interest in representing lifestyle and beauty brands. What this woman saw in me was something I couldn't see for myself at the time.

She ignited my passion for exploring public relations and pursuing what I had always wanted since graduating high school. I became a consultant and visionary for her skincare line that also sold at Bergdorf Goodman. She introduced me to her PR team, and I started learning the ins and outs of public relations at this firm in NYC. Eventually, the PR firm started representing my family's restaurant ZAVO in NYC for some time, and I was working for them on a referral basis. I had fostered strong relationships with publicists and journalists that helped propel my brand forward. Mirela is that woman every young woman should have in her life for inspiration, confidence, and friendship. She was a friend and a master connector who helped me get my foot in the door in a very competitive market.

The last step involves eliminating these beliefs through the tactics mentioned below:

- **Create an alternate belief.** Replace your negative thoughts with optimism and positivity. You don't have to aim for the moon and tackle everything at once. I dealt with one issue at a time. For example, speaking in front of many people was not my forte. But I began to think, *I hadn't spoken in front of a big audience before, but I've been talking to smaller groups of people for a long time.* I changed my perspective and used it to my advantage instead. By creating an alternate belief, I diverted my attention to something else that made me productive.

- **Challenge your beliefs.** Rather than reacting with fear, you can challenge your limiting beliefs intentionally. For me, it was confronting my doubts so that I could launch the first episode of my podcast. For you, it might be volunteering to spearhead a community event or pursuing a career you've always wanted despite your lack of experience. As you challenge your beliefs, you will begin to see various possibilities that prove your limiting beliefs to be false.

- **Choose a daily mantra.** Having a mantra can help boost your self-esteem and confidence. You become your cheerleader as you repeatedly say positive statements about yourself daily. When I think of the successful people I aspire to be, I ask myself, "Why not me? I am capable of everything and more. I can do this too!" By doing this every day, the mind resets and focuses on what you can achieve.

As you deal with your limiting beliefs one at a one, the way you think and react will change. Your mindset will shift to a different perspective. Then you will be more confident and ready than ever to manifest your beliefs in reality.

When you have confidence, you can turn your beliefs into reality. You have the power to make things happen—or not. It is up to you to bring your thoughts to fruition. As soon as you allow it, your new reality will manifest before you.

How? How do you manifest your desires and turn them into a reality? Is this possible? Can someone like you make that happen?

Yes!

The secret lies in what you think. Every belief can turn to reality when faith is applied.

You Are What You Think

The saying speaks for itself. The quality of your thoughts determines the quality of your life. You are responsible for creating a massive portion of your reality. You are the one writing your story, and that powerful story should resemble what you habitually think.

According to Napoleon Hill, "Whatever the mind can conceive and believe, it can achieve." His words perfectly resonate with the first pillar of turning your beliefs into reality. You must have strong willpower and imagination to manifest your vision.

Consider what it's like to apply for a job. It's perfectly normal for applicants to feel nervous before an interview. If you think you're not going to do well, you'll likely feel unconfident and conscious of your mistakes. You might stutter a lot, have a hard time understanding the questions, and make errors during the interview.

But if you're ready, confident, and poised, you will have a greater chance of landing that dream job of yours. By acknowledging what you think, you'll start to recognize how behavior patterns impact various situations—and then take charge! Be mindful of what you believe because what you think about consciously and subconsciously will soon manifest right before your eyes.

As the familiar saying goes, "Be careful what you wish for. You just might get it."

Empowerment

Speaking Your Power into Existence

*

Empowerment is authority. It's a signed permission slip to seize the day. It's the process of getting stronger and more confident and more engaged. To be empowered is to move through the world without fear or apology, and with these gifts, come an even deeper privilege-the ability to take charge of your own life and claim your rights.

— Oprah Winfrey

Having the ability to navigate life on your terms is the essence of empowerment. When you live an empowered life, you positively influence and impact the people around you. Napoleon Hill once said, "You are the master of your destiny. You can influence, direct, and control your environment. You can make your life what you want it to be." When you come into the fullness of who you are, you will inspire others and leave behind a powerful legacy that encourages people to follow in your footsteps.

I didn't always feel empowered. After my divorce, I tried picking up the pieces and living a fulfilling life with my son, but the stress got the best of me. At age 25, I was diagnosed with an autoimmune disease, alopecia. Before encountering this horrible disease, I didn't practice self-love. I couldn't wrap my head around it at first, but I knew this was a wake-up call. Doctors advised me to get steroids injected into my scalp, but they didn't warn me that it wouldn't treat the root cause of the problem. I knew if I went down this rabbit hole, my health would deteriorate even more.

I am fortunate to have family point me in the right direction, and my loving brother knew of an incredible holistic doctor who treated patients from his house. It was painful to lose my hair at such a young age, and my insecurities grew even more. At the time, I was working as a stylist and felt so conscious of my look. I couldn't go on working with my clients feeling aware of my problem.

I embarked on this holistic journey to find out the root cause of my autoimmune disease. I wasn't going to allow my health to be in someone else's hands. I say treat the root cause; otherwise, we are just suppressing the problem. I started to become empowered because I began meditating and visualizing for the first time. For the first time, I felt spiritually connected, my health started to improve, and my hair grew back within a few months, and I felt whole again. My life had changed forever when I met my holistic doctor from this tiny place in Queens. I incorporated studying Eastern holistic methods daily as a preventative.

The next step to BEPIC is to learn how to connect with the higher source and become one with G-D. I met my spiritual mentor, Michelle Berk, who introduced me to chanting. The power of sound and effect was a game-changer for me; it empowered me to learn how to speak into existence. I learned how to change my body's frequency so I could operate at a higher vibration. I finally understood the power of manifestation, and my healing started to happen so fast that my hair grew back naturally without any more steroids. I no longer had an autoimmune disease that could control me. I am grateful that I met this wonderful woman at my lowest when I was lost and confused about my purpose and mission in life. Michelle introduced me to the SGI center in NYC. My life changed instantly from the inside out by discovering a high-vibrational chant that originated from Nichiren Buddhism. I witnessed many Rabbis and other traditional Jews who benefited from chanting to the sound and effect. From the Buddhist perspective, sound and voice have great significance. The chant rewired my brain and empowered my voice.

How, then, can you become an empowered individual? How can you achieve your goals and not someone else's? How do you live the life you've always wanted?

Changing your beliefs about yourself and adopting positive behaviors can help you feel more empowered. By increasing your self-awareness, you will become conscious of how you think and react in different situations. When you are mindful in this way, you will also better understand your strengths and weaknesses. If you want to achieve your goals, you have to look deeply into yourself. Are your thoughts and actions aligned with the behavior needed to accomplish your goals? If not, you have to make the necessary changes.

People who have strong self-awareness learn from past experiences, which helps them make prudent decisions to improve their lives. At the same time, they know how to control their urges and recognize their limits. They usually don't have problems asking for guidance or help from others. Great thought leaders and influential public speakers are perfect examples of empowered individuals. Do you ever wonder why so many people listen to and believe in what they say? It's because they have tapped into their strengths and weaknesses. They already knew about their capabilities and searched for ways to improve their skills. They harnessed their power by increasing their self-awareness.

I feel the most empowered when I have high-energy people in my circle. I am lucky to be surrounded by savvy, driven, and powerful women who uplift others along the way. Creating strategic partnerships with exceptional influential leaders has always empowered me. Meeting the right key players can change a person's world one-eighty. One of these influential leaders is a powerhouse, Tobi Rubinstein, a master connector, a cancer survivor, and a bestselling author of The House of Faith and Fashion: What My Wardrobe Taught Me About G-D. Tobi's book resonated with me on a deeper level as I was a part of the fashion world for so long, and I understand how easy it is to be influenced and swayed when you are not spiritually empowered. Tobi seeks to uplift others and introduced me to Talia Rapps, the founder of The Spiritual Escape. Talia is a mastermind behind creating lasting memories and epic events globally for women, healthcare workers, and individuals. Together, as strategic partners, we are creating a brighter future for the next generation. The power is not what you know, but whom you know that can propel your business forward. These individuals don't lack authority; they have control and make decisions quickly, and have confidence in their ability to lead with authenticity. Their energies are infectious and uplift others mentally, spiritually, and emotionally. Remember, at the end of the day, wise women are never in competition with one another.

Personal Empowerment

The five steps to developing personal empowerment involve fundamental life changes, which means you have to be ready to welcome adjustments and get uncomfortable. Your path is not an easy process. It requires patience, readiness, and understanding to achieve the desired improvements. Here are the steps that can help you develop personal empowerment and establish your authority:

1. **Pursue a goal that involves having authority, such as becoming a leader or a manager.**

   Some examples include volunteering to take charge of a project or increasing your influence over planning your family's weekend getaway.

2. **Understanding the situation.**

   Knowing more about the upcoming event can help you plan for the next step. In the first example above, you might investigate more about the project and each group member's roles. As for the family getaway, take notes on what each member prefers and weigh in the options to help you create an effective plan.

3. **Reinforce your beliefs and improve your skills.**

First, you have to believe that you can achieve that specific goal. Take advantage of your strengths and work on your weaknesses so you have a greater chance of establishing your authority and power. Work on improving your skills by practicing and doing research.

4. **Take action and keep doing it.**

The first attempt won't always guarantee a smashing success. You have to be resilient and persistent, searching for other options to accomplish your goals when necessary.

5. **Evaluate your outcome.**

You might not see significant changes at first, but just keep going. Every small change counts. Assess the outcome and see if you played an essential role in making the plan a success. If it's not successful, there are plenty of opportunities in the future for you to try again. Over time, your influence grows until you can successfully establish your authority.

By focusing on what you can control and influence, you have a greater chance of reaching your goals. Move on to the next objective once you're finished. It will give you a sense of direction in life rather than a feeling of stagnation. Empowerment is about movement—you keep finding other ways to improve yourself and live an abundant life. In this way, you gain knowledge and experience that you can pass on to the next generation.

Speaking Your Power into Existence

Speaking your beliefs and desires into existence takes you one step closer to your dreams and goals. The truth is, the words we speak can take us to unimaginable heights. Words hold tremendous power that can make or break you.

Speaking up made me gain more confidence in myself. It made me feel empowered because, by becoming assertive, I gained control of the situation. I realized that I could be epic and do the things I've always wanted to do. Because of my growing self-esteem, I became capable of making sound decisions. Not long after, I earned the trust and respect of clients, subordinates, and fellow entrepreneurs because I knew what I wanted and how to get things done.

When you speak with passion and confidence about your ambitions, you take charge of your story. When you invest emotions and willpower into your aspirations, you give yourself the chance to realize the burning desire to turn belief into reality. Remember these principles:

- **Speak up, and the universe will listen.** A life filled with honesty and pure intention attracts power that helps realize desires. When you speak up, others will know your objectives. They might have the right connections and tools to help you attain the outcome.

- **Speak your mind, and your body will take action.** Speaking into existence is not just lip service. You have to walk the talk. The more you say something, the more you will find yourself ready to act.

- **Speak your thoughts into existence, and let everything fall into place.** Be that person who holds onto their purpose until it comes to fruition. Be the best version of yourself when you work and communicate. Excellence and success will follow, and so will your influence.

How we speak determines how we think, act, and attract into our lives. The power of words can build us up or destroy us. And that is our choice. Master the art of speaking into existence, and become an empowered individual ready to conquer anything!

Power

Gaining Power through Personal Satisfaction

*

Dream BIG...I mean REALLY BIG and on purpose! Women move mountains when aligned with something greater than themselves. The most amazing people reveal themselves and great things start showing up from every direction to support us on our path. What's even better is we become those amazing people that show up the same way for others. This is when magic happens.

—Loren Robin

What motivates you to keep pushing forward? What makes you whole and complete as an individual, entrepreneur, professional, or leader? Why do you do the things that you're doing? Napoleon Hill, my greatest inspiration, said, "The starting point of all achievement is DESIRE." The "why" motivates you to work harder and become more productive in various aspects of life. Your "why" dictates how you live your life and paves your way to success. But if you don't know why you're doing what you're doing, you won't achieve a sense of satisfaction and fulfillment. Without a sense of direction, you'll go around in circles and waste time and energy intended for growth and improvement.

Before starting my PR and digital branding boutique agency, I had a passion for designing a French-inspired luxury accessory line. This idea dawned on me while I was mentoring young girls in orphanages and high schools and first-year college students for the past three years. Out of my 1,500 mentees, Eliza stood out in the orphanage, wishing to wear beautiful French-inspired lace cuffs for her birthday. I had the burning desire to surprise her with a pair by making it for her. I always loved to draw and sketch different outfits as a child and aspired to become a designer. I decided to surprise her with my first pair of Jadore cuffs, and Eliza, to this day, wears them every year for her birthday. It marked the beginning of a luxury accessory line for charities where all proceeds will help young women feel confident and beautiful. The fashion industry was not new to me since I already owned a styling concierge business. Through mutual connections, I became acquainted with and friendly with Jonas Tamir, the SVP of Valentino-USA. He helped me gain exposure by using his showroom in the fashion district in NYC. In the Valentino showroom, I hosted events and brought brand awareness to the cause. I was fortunate enough to establish strategic partnerships with well-rounded individuals who supported my vision.

Everyone has a purpose in life—it's a matter of identifying that goal to obtain personal satisfaction. As you gain pride in the milestones you've reached, your power will increase. When that power accumulates over time, you can use it to your advantage and become more influential in your niche. Harnessing that capacity will enable you to do more and aim for a higher purpose—the following definition for yourself. This cycle goes on for infinity, inviting more change, growth, and an expanding list of remarkable achievements.

Take a good look at the big names in various industries—Oprah Winfrey, Whitney Wolfe, Elon Musk, Jeff Bezos, and many more. They have already reached the climax of their lives, yet they continue to do more. They search for other paths to explore and journey to places where few would go. They have curiosity, determination, and ideas they want to pursue until they can finally grasp it in their hands. They know why they're doing what they do. Even in the face of struggle, they persist and never stop reaching for the stars. The titans and the legends worldwide have lists of achievements that keep growing. They are driven, motivated, and inspired. Once they've accomplished their goals, they experience gratification—and want to pursue it again.

The moment I saw my path and found my purpose, I began to see the world differently. A purpose-driven life made my existence more meaningful and worthwhile. With that said, I felt satisfied and happy with the things I've achieved. The harder you work for something, the greater the gratification it brings once accomplished!

Success became sweeter and more profound because I worked hard to fulfill my ambitions.

What It Means

Personal satisfaction means something different to everyone. In my case, I felt satisfaction when I overcame my past and found my true identity, my true self. It took me years to find the root of my lack of confidence and frustration, but I increased my self-awareness and sought ways to improve myself. It helped me change my view on life, which enriched my mindset. I immersed myself in self-development books, performed meditation, listened to my favorite motivational speakers, and tuned to podcasts that enhanced my outlook on life.

For some people, personal satisfaction comes from other sources. It can come about by having happy relationships with family, friends, and colleagues, acquiring financial freedom, building a business, or attaining self-actualization. You don't have to achieve all of these goals at once. Instead, focus on the first one that comes to mind. Usually, this is the most crucial matter for you at the moment. Whatever it is, make sure that it is what you truly desire most.

Achieving Personal Satisfaction

Readiness is a criterion for success. List the steps you need to take to reach that goal, and then create your plan. Explore the options and scrutinize which can benefit you the most. Below are reminders that will guide you in the pursuit of attaining personal satisfaction.

- **Don't be afraid of failure.** Failure is the springboard to your forthcoming victories. Nobody has ever reached the top without making mistakes. The prominent figures mentioned above have all experienced loss. There is never a shortcut to success. The difference between the winners and losers is that winners never quit. They keep going, and so should you. They never find a reason to give up and take the time to understand and learn from failures.

- **Keep on innovating.** The world has myriad problems that need solutions from individuals like you. Providing a solution can serve as the supreme purpose that can lead you to personal satisfaction. Who knows, you might be the best answer to a pressing issue that everyone wants to address.

- **Do not allow yourself to stay stagnant.** If you no longer find satisfaction in what you're doing, you likely feel like you don't have a purpose anymore. Life becomes monotonous and less challenging, so you no longer enjoy the process or take as much joy in your accomplishments. It can be a trap where most people get stuck. The mistake is apparent. People who lose their sense of purpose stop when they achieve their goals. It should not happen to you. You need to keep moving forward if you want growth. The public figures mentioned above never stayed in one spot. They kept moving, searching for ways to innovate their brand while continuing to help people around the world.

Once you've obtained a goal, move on to the next "why" and then the next. In this way, you keep on growing, acquiring, and applying new knowledge and skills. Explore more spaces and try new things. Become a better version of yourself, and be a trailblazer in your niche. Keep on finding your satisfaction to harness the power that can change lives and impact the world.

Tips for Small Businesses

Without publicity and a well-known reputation, a business may have a hard time growing and thriving in its respective industry. A steady stream of efficient strategies can help build an audience that equates to more profit.

Public relations can help develop, promote and manage brand reputation. A common misconception that many small-time business owners believe is that PR is for large corporations and globally recognized brands. As a PR consultant for many years, I often correct this notion. PR isn't only limited to million-dollar companies. All types of businesses can benefit from public relations if performed appropriately.

Because of PR, I've witnessed how small entrepreneurs started from humble beginnings and progressively scaled into successful and sought-after brands. Here are five reasons to invest and plan your business growth with PR.

1. **Create brand recognition through a step-by-step process.** It takes time, plenty of brainstorming, and research to formulate the best approaches for your business to get recognized. Whether you have recently launched your brand or have been in the industry for a while, investing in PR can help you achieve your business goals. You don't have to spend a fortune and in bulk when it comes to PR. If you choose to partner with a PR firm, packages are often available that don't constraint your budget as a small-time business owner. There are also simple steps you can take to get started on your own.

2. **Promote your brand image and values.** I believe the most vital element that a brand should obtain from the target audience is trust. Without

trust, it's harder to attain an increase in exposure and following. The lack of credibility can eventually lead to failure for the brand to grow and loss of sales. Through video marketing, thought leadership pieces, specialized events, and more, public relations can help bridge the business and the target consumers.

3.   **Make connections.** You can gain access to a vast web of influencers and other relationships that potentially help your brand reputation grow. Cross marketing is an example in which you can partner with other companies that complement your brand. By creating conditions favorable for your target market, both parties can benefit from this partnership.

4.   **Influence the market in your favor.** With a cleverly crafted story that focuses on your brand, you can seize the audience's attention and connect with them on a personal level. PR's job is to change and influence the public's way of thinking about your brand. Positive messages relevant to the

audience help elicit good responses. In certain situations where a crisis is inevitable, PR can turn the tide and fix your brand's image.

5. **Improve and strengthen your brand's relationship with the community.** By being active and becoming involved with the local community, can amplify your chances of recognition. Charities and fundraising events can help positively impact your brand and build your business's reliability. More consumers may turn to your brand and offer their support by forming ties with the local market.

How To Get Started

Small businesses can begin with simple strategies to build their PR efforts and progress to grander campaigns as time passes. To get started, here are some tips that business owners can apply when it comes to PR.

• **Set your goals.** It's vital to have an established purpose from the start to know where you're going.

The more specific your objectives are, the better. What do you want to achieve? Which consumers benefit the most from your product or service? The answers to these questions can serve as a good foundation for a public relations strategy.

- **Know your audience and create a connection.** Identifying your target audience can make it easier for you to establish your reach. Knowing where to find your market is a good start. Make sure to keep connected with your audience by being consistent and reliable to show that you're genuine. In return, you may gain customers' trust and confidence in your business, which is the ultimate goal of PR.

- **Strengthen your customer service.** People love coming back to places where they're happy and satisfied. It's the job of business owners to set a standard for excellent service that assures customer satisfaction. Keeping your customer happy should be the bottom line.

- **Measure the outcome of your strategies.** Knowing what worked well can help you determine which methods were effective. Some campaigns succeed while some don't. These results are valuable and serve as your guide in tweaking your approaches in future campaigns.

Public relations can make a company stand firmly on its foundation while overcoming any obstacle. With the proper tools and methods for boosting brand reputation and publicity, any business can thrive regardless of its size. PR strategies may differ, but the goal is to create a mutual connection between the business brand and the public, which can pave the way to increased sales and profit. For small business owners, the opportunities that PR offers can be beneficial and optimal for growth. By prioritizing PR, entrepreneurs can change the future of their businesses.

Inner Voice

Finding Your Unique Voice & Speak Up

*

A world where girls are valued, because they must be, they have so much to contribute, and that's the economic opportunity that the world is missing. And then a world where a woman's voice really makes a difference. Because we have a different set of values, and if we speak them and live them, then the world will reflect that. And that's bound to be a more equitable and just place.

-Pat Mitchell, Former President and CEO of PBS

Now that you have the desired qualities of an entrepreneur and an empowered individual, the next step is to gain a foothold in your niche by finding your unique voice. But in a sea of competition, it's easy to get lost and feel invisible. How can you compete against a hundred competitors? How do you stand out in a crowd? Can you successfully find your voice in the market?

The path to becoming a successful entrepreneur may be daunting, but if it means reaching the top and obtaining widespread authority, then the price is worth it. There were many times when I just wanted to speak up but self-sabotaged myself. I felt that my message would not resonate with others and that I wasn't credible enough. I had to find my inner strength and voice to believe in my abilities. I had to step out of my comfort zone and decide that I am an expert in my niche and decided I needed to hire mentors that helped me in public speaking, business coaching, and media training.

Being a college dropout increased my insecurities, but I didn't let my lack of a degree become a deciding factor in whether or not I'd achieve success. I started interning for a PR firm in New York City and fostered relationships with publicists and journalists who helped propel my brand forward. I taught myself everything I needed to know, in addition to my incredible media guru Amy Rosenblum, who inspired me to leap of faith in the mass media. By the end of the year, I learned the ins and outs of public relations and decided to step to a whole new level. In 2017, I bootstrapped ZavoMedia Group with only five thousand dollars, passion, and a spirit of determination. I realized that anything is possible as long as you believe in yourself. Anything is attainable as long as you put your heart into it.

Bear in mind, however, that running a business is easier said than done. Anyone can aspire to reach for the stars, but only a few can build a rocket to get there. We've heard of entrepreneurs with promising businesses that fell short only a few years later. In the face of defeats like this, it's easy to give up. Only those who are resilient, resourceful, and creative remain in the arena. For every renowned brand that's thrived for decades, there's an intelligent and hardworking CEO.

So, what's their secret? What made losers quit while winners bask in the limelight of success? Most aspiring entrepreneurs don't realize that running a business isn't as easy as counting one, two, three. It involves peeling back multiple layers before getting to the center. Managing a business isn't only about the profits and expenditures or the number of customers year after year. It isn't just about creating a new line of products or services to entice more followers. It's also about dealing with the punches aimed at the company. No matter how good the plans are, they won't matter if the one in charge—you—lack the qualities needed to redirect criticism, fight back, and dodge when trouble appears.

This adaptability comes from within—the inner core. You have to start internally before moving outward. How can you handle stressful situations in your company if you can't handle yourself first? That's a question worth asking. You have to cultivate your inner strength and capabilities to harness your power. Without complete control of yourself and your business, you may not last long in the industry.

Let's look again at the lives of some well-known, successful figures who have inspired me—Oprah Winfrey, Sara Blakely, Barbara Corcoran, and others. None of them started with fame and fortune. Behind each of their victories, there's hard work, perseverance, dedication, and self-discipline. These successful CEOs were all not seen and not heard at some point before reaching the top. Even at a disadvantage, they still used their unique voice to speak up because they were determined to see things through. Knowing that even the most successful people have faced upsets and obstacles has sustained me through my struggles.

Without a mentor or someone to guide me through the challenges in life, I found it difficult to traverse to the other side. It then sparked an idea. I thought, *Wouldn't it be great if women could have someone to look up to, someone who could teach them how to unlock their authoritative voice and harness their power?* This question led me to my inner voice, which told me to become a source of strength for other women seeking to do amazing things.

I created a podcast platform where I interview executive female entrepreneurs and mentors who offer success tips and tricks to women as they embark on their entrepreneurship journeys. My podcast, *What Makes a Woman*, turned out to be a massive success, and I gained knowledge and experience from the legends, C-level executives, and professionals who came on my show.

I wanted a platform where I could have thoughtful and inspirational conversations with women from various backgrounds and challenge the status quo. As a result, the secrets and stories of success that these multifaceted and diverse women share have motivated listeners worldwide to step up and own their influence.

This platform gave me a voice that made me stand out as a digital storyteller, and in time I became a beacon of light and inspiration to aspiring entrepreneurs around the world. I successfully established myself as an expert in my niche and have since helped more than 1,500 young girls and women through my leadership academy.

It is my turn to pass down the knowledge—to inspire you to believe in your strength to succeed, speak your power into existence, take action, and embrace the confidence that's for you. Working on your inner core will help you obtain your unique inner voice. As soon as your voice stands out, you'll achieve success sooner than you think.

Entrepreneurial Spirit

An entrepreneur must possess certain qualities and traits to gain respect for what you do. Take a look at the prominent names in the business industry. What sets them apart? They possess authenticity, consistency, and adaptability.

As a result, they have established authority. It created more traction for brands and more connections with other influential personalities. These qualities can help you propel yourself to greater heights. As long as you remain open-minded to change and evolution, it's safe to say that you're on the right track. These guidelines will keep you on track:

- **Be authentic.** Being genuine in what you do and say makes a huge difference; it's no longer about lip service. Furthermore, never forget to put value into your relationship with your customers. They like to stay connected with brands that listen to what they say and suggest—it's because they trust in your business.

- **Be consistent.** Consistency makes your business reliable. When consumers see you stand by your word, they will invest more energy in your industry, knowing yours is a brand to trust. When you're consistent, you show passion and dedication in satisfying the needs of your customers.

- **Be adaptable.** Some businesses struggle to keep up with ever-changing trends. However, moving with the trends is the only way to stay connected with potential clients. If you remain outdated and out of topic, your followers will lose interest. They will find it harder to connect with something stuck in the past. By adapting to modern tools like social media, people see that you value your connection with them.

Finding the Unique Inner Voice

How do you stand out in the crowd? It is a big challenge for entrepreneurs with tight competition. You have to find ways to set yourself apart. One of the best ways to do this is to gain a unique voice that everyone will easily remember.

When I started my career as an entrepreneur, I never stopped learning. I read books, listened to podcasts, attended conferences, and followed the work of my favorite motivational speakers. Knowing I'd overcome the mistakes I made in the past gave me the courage to dive into different industries, and soon I found the niche that was right for me.

One after another, I accomplished many milestones because I kept on moving toward the next goal while harnessing the unique voice that made me stand out in my field. Through these steps, I laid a strong foundation and built my way up. To help you succeed, I'd like to share these tips for discovering your inner voice and working on your path to success:

- **Brand yourself.** Without proper branding, you're just another business. You have to establish your name in your industry. To achieve that, you must invest in good brandings, such as a striking name, logo, slogan, and more. Memorable branding establishes your identity and leaves a long-lasting impression on people. When you hear words like Coca-Cola, Nike, and Versace, what comes to mind? You think about their catchy slogans, logos, and colors. They are more than just names. Now it's your turn to have that effect on your market.

- **Find your mission.** A life without a purpose is dull and empty and deprives a person of fulfillment and meaning. It is also true for businesses; they need a reason to exist. One of the main goals of your branding should be to convey your mission, not only to drive your business forward but to make you appear more appealing, human, and responsible. A mission will help you attract even more supporters to your brand. A task that allows you to give back to the community and your followers is always a good idea. After all, without their support, you wouldn't be where you are today.

- **Own your influence.** Owning your power means embracing your strengths and weaknesses as an individual and as a leader. By showing who you are, people see and appreciate the hard work you've done for your brand and the community. Use your influence to spark change, instigate action, and catalyze others to become better. Your unique voice becomes a part of you through these actions, making it easier for people to identify you.

- **Collaborate.** Be open to possibilities. Collaboration with other influencers helps expand your reach. Even if you're starting at the community level, your business can still garner attention and publicity if you team up with another brand. Just make sure both parties benefit from this partnership. Use your platform to uplift others, and in return, others will also lift you.

When you've discovered your unique inner voice, use it to your advantage to stand out and propel yourself forward. You'll seem irreplaceable once you're recognized. According to Darren Prince and Patrick Bet-David, both rockstar entrepreneurs, millionaires, and *Wall Street Journal* best-selling authors who guested on my show, making yourself irreplaceable is a decisive advantage.

Make yourself so hard to replace that the market can't afford to get rid of you. As a result, your value goes up, no matter what the situation is. The moment you decide to be unique and different, you begin to stand out and gain recognition like never before.

Courage

Developing the Courage to Become the Number 1 Authority

*

Be fearless. Have the courage to take risks. Go where there are no guarantees. Get out of your comfort zone even if it means being uncomfortable. The road less traveled is sometimes fraught with barricades, bumps, and uncharted terrain. But it is on that road where your character is truly tested and has the courage to accept that you're not perfect, nothing is, and no one is—and that's OK.
—Katie Couric, Journalist and Talk-Show Host

Nothing happens if you don't dare to leap. Some decisions in life require guts and audacity. You have to step out of your comfort zone. If you don't take action, nothing happens. You remain stagnant and nestled in your comfort until you realize it's already too late to take a step. Sharon Lechter, a business mentor, co-author of *Rich Dad Poor Dad*, editor of Napoleon Hill's *Outwitting the Devil,* and author of *Think and Grow Rich for Women*, talked about fear becoming our own worst enemy. On my show, she warned that fear holds us back. There is nothing to fear but fear itself. Understanding the importance of our goals raises the self-confidence that helps us conquer our fears.

You need the courage to be epic and to rise above the competition. You have to learn to embrace the ups and downs in life. You have to remember to take the good with the bad wherever you go. Mistakes and failures are inevitable. Instead of fearing them, experience them to become stronger.

I remember the words of Napoleon Hill that created an impact in my life: "When defeat comes, accept it as a signal that your plans are not sound, rebuild those plans, and set sail once more toward your coveted goal."

Imagine that you're a seed planted deep down the soil, aspiring to grow into a healthy plant that flowers and bears fruit. But that can't happen all at once. You're still in that contained, earthen space. Days pass by, but you're still down there in the dark, cold, and quiet. When will you see the sunlight? Is there even the slightest chance that you'll see a ray from the sun? Depressing thoughts flood your mind, drowning your positivity. Maybe it's better to remain this way, all cooped up in this little space.

But you decide not to stay trapped—because you're resilient. You muster the courage to rise and put yourself out there. A tiny plant breaks through the soil. Now, you're basking under the glorious sunlight—the warmth you've been longing to have. Sturdier than ever, you emerge victorious after conquering your doubts and fears. Like a seed, you have the power to become epic. Change your mindset from scarcity to abundance.

When you have courage, you can confidently put yourself out there and experience all that life offers. Through each challenge you face, you learn more about your strengths and weaknesses. By courageously moving forward, you get to live and write your history using your own words and not someone else's. When you have courage, you can step into the spotlight, no longer overshadowed by others.

It doesn't matter how old you are or your whereabouts. Nothing happens if you don't have courage. It's up to you to make that decision—to take that next step. The road may not be easy, but when you're willing to take risks and brave the storms, you have a greater chance of success. It's certainly better than doing nothing at all.

There is no learning and growth without some difficulty and struggle. If you want to become epic, you need to keep on risking failure. You have to keep moving forward and become the number one authority in your niche.

Become an Expert

Once you've mustered that courage, you're on your way to greatness. When people see your confidence, they'll start to listen to what you say. They'll pay attention to your advice because you will have grown into a credible expert in your niche.

Confidence is like a muscle that needs practice. It takes believing in your abilities and potential. *Believe it and become it* instead of *fake it until you make it*. I wasn't always confident because I was afraid to speak my mind as a teenager. I thought my views and beliefs would alienate me from others. But when I changed my mindset and conquered my fears and doubts, I realized that I could do epic things.

Below are the key lessons I've learned over more than a decade of entrepreneurship. You, too, can become a recognized expert in your niche by applying the following methods:

- **Specialize and niche down.** You can serve everybody, but you can't please everybody. There will always be someone who won't be satisfied with your product or service. Choosing a niche means targeting one's messaging to a specific group rather than a general audience. Rather than being a jack-of-all-trades, narrow down into a niche where your skills can shine. Find ways to succeed in that craft until nobody knows it better than you. People tend to listen to experts who know best. If you're one of them, people will flock to you and ask for your advice. In this way, clients will know where to look. By becoming a specialist, you will stand out with your acquired skills and experience.

- **Always provide valuable content.** Position yourself as a professional who constantly supplies others with reliable information. When people acknowledge you as a valuable source of knowledge, there's a good chance that you can go viral, thus increasing your reputation as an expert. Free courses, e-books, and webinars are great ways to offer value and show off your expertise to people curious to learn more about you. Just bear in mind that the content produced must be valid and dependable. Doing research and double-checking your sources is vital for keeping your authority intact. Providing untrue information can put your expert status in jeopardy. But once people know that you offer trustworthy information and valuable content, they will be willing to obtain what you sell, no matter the price. That's how powerful your authority can become.

- **Be visible.** Publicity is how anyone can gain recognition. If you don't put yourself out there, how will other people know about your business? How do you gain traction with your brand? Especially in the digital age, you need to stay visible and establish your presence on social media. With many social media platforms available, startup entrepreneurs are often confused about where to begin. Luckily, you don't have to take advantage of every outlet. You can choose one or two platforms to use to market your products and services. Focus on where you'd like to promote your business and connect with your supporters.

- **Get seen in renowned publications.** Earning the public's trust requires hard work and dedication. Along the way, you'll face criticism that challenges your authenticity and authority as an expert. One way to overcome the noise is to gain credibility through other reliable channels, such as those published in reputable media outlets or magazines.

To start, take advantage of your local newspaper, and make connections with journalists and editors. These brands have years of credibility and influence, making it hard for anyone to question their integrity.

Most readers and patrons expect them to provide quality journalism. Once your target market sees your name published on paper (whether physical or digital), their impression of you will change dramatically.

Once you have established an influence, maximize all the opportunities. Engage with your audience, and be authentic when conversing with them so that you can successfully position yourself as the number one authority in your niche.

Landing Consistent Media Opportunities

Create Visibility, Credibility & Profitability

*

Beyond our borders, having societies empower and unleash the brainpower of over half the world's population is a benefit to us all. Leaders must use both hard and soft power, but now more than ever, they must be able to connect with those around them. Their followers are now their stakeholders, so today's leaders have to encourage collaborations while making decisions that support their vision and priorities on a global stage.

—Moira Forbes, Publisher of FORBES WOMAN

Public Relations

From a public relations strategist's point of view, there are four things you need to pay attention to if you want to achieve the proper exposure: visibility, consistency, credibility, and profitability.

Visibility means being seen and heard by the public through various media outlets: the internet, television, newspaper, radio, podcasts, and magazines. You gain a tremendous amount of exposure through these platforms.

Don't ever hesitate to grab these opportunities when presented. Even if you only have a slight chance to get featured, seize those offers. They can boost your visibility in the market. Coming up with unique strategies can help capture media attention. Today's trend is to go viral with a fantastic story in tow. It can give you ample exposure to curious eyes around the world.

I have published my story on *Forbes, Huffington Post, Entrepreneur,* and other publications. I talked about how my confidence and vulnerability led me to become a media mogul in those features. I also took that opportunity to share tips and lessons I've learned throughout my journey.

The result has been phenomenal. My visibility skyrocketed and helped me gain more clients than before. People became more interested in my brand after seeing my success through these media outlets.

Consistency speaks for itself. Be consistent with your voice, and don't change your image too often. It's vital to stick to your vision and mission to the end to show that you're serious about achieving your goals.

Consistency, in this context, is about maintaining your image and voice throughout your campaign so your audience can easily find your brand and distinguish it from others. Although trends change, you can still adapt and ride the tide. Just make sure not to lose your voice and forget why your business exists in the first place.

Credibility refers to social proof. It means your business performs and responds well in different situations. One way to determine your business's reputation is to see how often you have exposure in forums, discussion boards, and trending topics.

When others talk about your business, they give a free boost to your reputation. Taking advantage of this word-of-mouth phenomenon is one of the oldest and most effective tactics in increasing exposure. Even better, it's free!

Sometimes, however, criticism and negative reviews can stain your brand and affect your reputation. The best way to go about this is to address the problem. Be humble enough to acknowledge your mistakes, and show sincerity by resolving issues with the correct compensation.

Holding your ground and defending yourself might seem the valid route if you believe the dispute will go away on its own and become forgotten. An unhealed wound to your reputation can fester and become too difficult to fix later on. It's best to tackle issues like this as soon as possible. It also shows how reliable and dedicated you are in solving problems that involve your brand.

Profitability is the ultimate marker of how successful you are on your journey as an entrepreneur.

People flock and keep coming back to brands with high sales because others enjoy your products and services.

As a consumer, what brands do you consider when choosing a product or service? One factor is profitability because it means it has been tried and tested by the public. Increased visibility, credibility, and reliability lead directly to profitability.

When you practice the four principles above, you'll land remarkable opportunities. When people see you as a trusted and dependable brand, they will see you as a light to guide them in a storm.

When you're visible, consistent, and reliable, many people will talk about your brand, providing more attention to your name. Thus, this domino effect increases your profitability as it draws in more attention from curious minds.

Personal Branding

In six years, I transitioned from being a celebrity stylist and designer to the CEO of my public relations and digital branding agency in NYC. It wasn't easy, but I have learned many valuable lessons on grit, determination, and passion throughout my life that helped get me to where I am today and that I believe can help other entrepreneurs.

- **Overcome adversities with self-acceptance.** When I was a child, my family fled from the Soviet Union and settled as refugees in Vienna, Austria, for five years. I became fascinated with the diverse European culture, and it was there that I discovered my true love for art and design. I then found my dream to be in the world of beauty, couture and fashion.

After immigrating to the U.S. when I was older, my father sustained the family as a restaurateur. I looked up to my father and aspired to follow in his footsteps someday. Soon, I became a parent myself at 19 years old, and after going through a divorce, I had to raise my son as a single parent. I strived to be a good role model for him. As a college dropout and a single mother, I juggled freelance jobs while dealing with failures and financial problems.

But one day, I decided to end this misery and took small, consistent steps to change and improve myself. I reinvented myself by reading self-development books and listening to groundbreaking and motivational speakers. I learned to practice gratitude every single day, meditate, and let go of my past, and I began to see life in a new light.

Your story might not be the same as mine, but we all must overcome adversity as an entrepreneur. Accept your weaknesses and find ways to develop yourself to move forward.

- **Find your mission.** Over time, I gained victories and made my name in show business as a stylist and designer. I lived the dream: I hosted fashion brunches with top designers at my family's restaurant ZAVO NYC, attended fashion shows worldwide, and my luxury accessory designs featured in high-end fashion showrooms in Paris and New York. However, I soon started feeling that this couldn't be it. I was part of an external world, and it didn't give me long-term satisfaction.

When traveling to 5-star hotels in NYC, I had to style all types of clients. I remember when my client's daughter was devastated because her parents wanted her to go the traditional route and not follow her dreams. This moment changed my whole perspective and outlook.

Although this career brought me joy and opportunities to work in fashion and travel the world, I realized it didn't help the voiceless and the next generation. I wanted to tap into my purpose. I decided to pivot and reinvent myself to reach my higher goal by becoming a mentor and a digital storyteller.

From my perspective, stagnancy impedes growth. Everyone can grow and create more extensive results for the greater good. If you feel that something is missing, look inside yourself and find out why. You might discover another new meaning to your life, and finding that mission could be your path to ultimate happiness.

- **Own your influence.** As a young girl, I didn't have enough confidence and mentors to guide me through life. Once I had the resources, I decided to address this dilemma through my podcast. I envisioned a platform where successful female entrepreneurs could pass down their knowledge, share stories and inspire fellow women.

One of the most impactful experiences I've had so far was when I dedicated a month on my podcast to Black Lives Matter and highlighting Black women entrepreneurs who are disruptors. I was able to use my role to help empower other women, regardless of background.

Through this experience, I felt I could impact others' lives and support women who might not have had the opportunity to share their stories previously. Everyone should embrace their rich heritage and become fearless in entering the arena. I believe that to be the true power of a strong woman.

I encourage entrepreneurs to use their platforms to uplift other voices and create circumstances that give others chances to propel forward. From my perspective, a person's most outstanding achievement is when you believe in someone with all that you have and help amplify their voice so that they can use it boldly and freely.

- **Always be professional.** Earlier this year, the world's economy dwindled because of Covid-19. Businesses were affected and forced to furlough employees or declare bankruptcy, leaving millions of people jobless. I was fortunate enough to continue paying my team, taking on more women freelancers, and guiding entrepreneurs on approaching marketing today.

However, it's tough to navigate times of uncertainty as a business leader, and it can be especially challenging to respond to negative feedback when facing such a difficult time.

Through my time in the PR space, I know that it's essential to constantly learn from clients' feedback as an entrepreneur rather than taking it personally and letting your emotions get in the way. Let that criticism inform how your company will evolve in the future. Apologize to your customer for their experience, and take steps to improve.

- **Keep unfolding new chapters.** As long as entrepreneurs continue to evolve, I believe more opportunities will come knocking at the door. Don't be afraid to pursue new roles because the world is ever-changing. It is time to become more confident and be proud of your achievements — big or small.

Accept your vulnerabilities, and use your confidence to overcome difficulties in life. As for me, I will persist in inspiring women to strive for success, hoping that this will create more ripples to prepare the next generation of successful women entrepreneurs. We are all meant for greatness.

Challenges of Personal Branding

No matter who you are, your brand is your new superpower. Don't underestimate the power of your online presence. I am a big proponent of gaining the proper visibility, credibility, and profitability through storytelling. Your unique story is your biggest differentiator that will set you apart from your competitors. Keep in mind that people don't buy products; they buy stories—every professional needs to establish a trust factor with clients and strategic partnerships based on their online presence.

Personal branding remains a vital aspect of entrepreneurship that requires thoughtful planning. To attract your target audience and increase sales, you need to cultivate an authentic presence that aligns well with your brand's mission and core values. The following are the five concerns that challenge businesses when it comes to personal branding.

The first is creating a ***core statement*** to catch the audience's attention. Understanding your mission and focus must be on the top of the list. What is it that you offer, and how can you help solve your market's problems? What sets you apart from other businesses? These questions are some of the primary points you have to cover in making your accurate statement. Most importantly, make your core message clear and concise. It lets people see your true intentions and straightforwardness without beating around the bush.

Second, having a ***broader standpoint*** makes you more flexible and relevant. Your industry is ever-changing, which means you have to stay updated with the trends that come and go. Keeping an open eye on these things makes it easier for you to adapt and efficiently address concerns that your brand can take advantage of over a certain period. Entrepreneurs who fail to catch up with the times encounter difficulty retaining clients and earning new ones.

Third, displaying your ***expertise*** entices your audience. People seek expert opinions and are eager to find reliable sources of advice. Specializing in a niche helps you stand out because your audience recognizes your mastery and expertise. Skilled and competent brands are hard to come by. An established presence as an expert shows how effective you are at solving a specific set of problems that nobody else can.

Fourth, **connecting with your audience** shows your value and authenticity. People appreciate brands that take the time to listen and communicate with their followers. Technology has made everything more convenient. Technology has become pivotal in helping unknown brands to gain popularity and recognition.

Lastly, **rebranding** can be a total headache. While it is not uncommon for companies to reinvent themselves, entrepreneurs may think rebranding is risky. At my communications and media boutique agency, we guide our clients and help them identify where to invest their energy.

Digital storytelling is an effective intervention as you transition from the old to the new scheme. The power of personal branding draws more interest and gains more trust whether you are a professional, entrepreneur, social impact brand, or small business. People buy stories, not products.

Understanding these elements of building your brand will help solidify your presence in your industry. By following these tips, you can achieve promising results that propel you upward.

Setting Yourself Up for Success: 10 Tips for Aspiring Entrepreneurs

The mantra of my success comes from the failures that were defeated time and again. My life is not perfect, and I have confronted countless struggles before reaching my zenith. When I was young, I looked up to successful people and used their stories as my inspiration.

I adopted valuable lessons and qualities from these significant individuals to break through the glass ceiling and achieve success. Here are the ten best pieces of career advice for aspiring entrepreneurs and thought leaders who aim for the top.

1. Learning is the first step.

As humans, we are prone to making mistakes in life. We settle the score by learning from our faults and developing better habits. But why do we keep on making the same mistakes over again? It is because we refuse to learn. When we start to acknowledge our lapses, we can move forward and become better individuals.

2. You are powerful beyond measure.

People told me that I should conform to what society dictates me to do and be a woman. But I did not let the words of others define who I am. I know my capabilities as a woman, and I am confident about what I can do to serve my community. Do not let limitations and doubts cloud your confidence because you are more than what people say. Believe in yourself that you can do it.

3. Gratitude makes us appreciate different perspectives.

When you start being grateful, you begin to see things in a new light. I used to see gloomy days ahead because of the problems that drained my energy. As I practiced the value of gratitude, I started to feel more positive and invigorated. Being thankful for the blessings I receive daily encouraged me to work harder. I ended up happier and more content with what I had rather than stressing over things beyond my control.

4. When you feel lost, go back to your "why."

In a world full of distractions, we undoubtedly go astray and lose sight of our goals. It is vital to stay rooted in your purpose by reminding yourself consistently why you do what you do. I desired to gain more knowledge and develop my talents because I wanted to educate and empower the next generation of female entrepreneurs. At times of doubt, I looked back to where I started. It helped me evoke the passion I felt when I commenced my mission.

5. Failure is the foundation of success.

We tend to perceive failure as a heavy downfall. Therefore, we try to avoid it by playing safe or doing nothing at all. Taking risks is an inevitable part of the journey if you want to be successful. If we fail, we can stand up and try again. I failed many times when I started my business, but I refused to stay defeated. My failures became my stepping stones which helped me climb the ladder to success.

6. Seize the moment.

Cliché as it may sound, it is the truth. Nothing comes to fruition if we do not take action. Doing our best every day brings in positive results rather than doing things half-heartedly. Opportunities come when we least expect them. Hence, it is crucial to be ready and seize the chance when it presents.

I create a checklist daily to see my progress and acquire more skills to improve myself. Preparation is key to grasping opportunities.

7. Be adaptable and stay relevant to the situation.

Last year was a challenging time for everyone, but it revealed other directions to achieve their wins. The ability to switch directions according to the changes gives us the advantage of being at the forefront. I have managed to pull through and avert the crisis by staying relevant to the times. I modified my methods of handling my business to stay connected with my clients. If we remain stuck in the old ways, it will be harder to keep up with the trend.

8. Always know people are rooting for you.

Never let the noise pull you down rock bottom. You may not seem to notice it straight away, but some still support and believe in you till the end. Instead of stressing over the people you can't please, turn to those ready to hold your hand. Never take these individuals for granted because they are vital to helping you reach your goals.

9. The sun doesn't shine every day; there are rainy days, too.

Life goes up and down whether we like it or not. There are good and bad days; it is a matter of taking the good with the bad. It is never a smooth walk in the park, but it does not mean we have to give up searching. I also had bad days, but they did not hinder me from fulfilling my mission. I made sure to keep moving forward and enjoy the journey instead. Tomorrow is another chance to start over and become better.

10. There is a time for everything.

Age and gender are not the ultimate barriers that stop us from attaining our dreams. It is our self-limiting beliefs. Renowned billionaires, celebrities, and thought leaders reached the pinnacle at different phases of their lives. It took me years to establish myself as an expert in my niche, but I never let these factors become obstacles in my path.

These career tips can serve as a guide in building yourself to the top. Most importantly, let us not forget that family is an essential aspect of our lives. Family can be a great source of inspiration and motivation to keep us pushing forward. Remember that life is a marathon and not a sprint. It is a matter of time when you take charge and design your life the way you want it.

Five Tips for Launching a Successful Startup

Creating a business from scratch involves a detailed, thorough preparation, design, research, and strategy. But challenging as it may be, getting your business off the ground is possible. As a business owner myself, I understand the struggles that novices go through, so I hope to provide clarity and guidance.

The following are the five key takeaways I've learned in creating and fostering a brand that I believe can be helpful to aspiring entrepreneurs.

1. Create a brand based on your vision, mission, and goals.

Several business owners often overlook the importance of good branding, which results in a rocky start. It might seem basic and easy, but it's more than just thinking up a catchy name. A good brand possesses the ability to connect and communicate with your target consumers, thus creating a brand relationship with your audience. It is no longer about what you want for the brand but rather how the public perceives and receives your brand in their lives.

Your brand also serves as the first and best representative of your business, so it should have a personality that consumers easily remember. Through this personality, your brand's values and culture need to shine through. Determine your company's vision and mission statement, and set a goal for your startup. It can help you develop your brand's personality and, in turn, enable your audience to identify their roles as consumers of your brand.

In my experience as a branding expert, consumers begin to appreciate a brand when they see more success with your product compared to your competitors. As a result, they will become living proof of your brand's value, as their patronage and support can help your business grow. However, I believe this is only achievable if you've created the right brand — one based on a clear vision, mission, and goal from the start.

2. Find the social media strategy that works for you — and perfect it.

After successful branding, it's time to take the next step: strategic marketing through social media. Social media is an effective avenue for building networks and reaching out to people from all walks of life. Take advantage of this to reap fantastic results. The best way to connect with the audience is to engage and talk with them; online, you can find out more about what your consumers enjoy and want to have in the future.

However, not all forms of social media provide the best solution for every business. Finding the right social media strategy for your startup boils down to recognizing the demographics of your target audience. What platforms can you find your target demographic on? What types of content are capturing their attention?

The use of other marketing tools like ads and campaigns can help your brand gain more reach and exposure. I've found that investing in good copy and eye-catching graphic design can also increase engagement and bring in revenue. After seeing the most effective method, make necessary improvements to be the best in the field.

3. Create video content.

Consumers want video content. Nowadays, videos and infographics are some of the easiest ways to catch people's attention. Why is that? From my perspective, it takes more energy to skim through an article, no matter how informative and valuable the content might be.

As a result, videos take the spotlight because they are more accessible and convenient from the audience's point of view. Seize this opportunity to create quality videos that showcase your brand's personality, provide relevant and valuable content, and build trust among current and potential customers.

When creating your video content, I recommend taking a different approach to help set your business apart from the competition. For instance, when appropriate, you can use humor to relate to your audience or take on an informative and educational tone to build authority. I've also observed many brands that share inspirational messaging to help motivate their audience. Take on human personality traits within your communications and videos. I've found this is essential to stand out from the rest.

4. Be dependable.

After setting the brand personality, always stick to what your brand represents. It indicates stability and dependability and creates a clear image of your brand's offerings inside the consumer's mind. Nobody would want a business that is contradicting itself, ambiguous, and all over the place.

At the same time, consistency should go hand in hand with authenticity. People can spot when a business is disingenuous. To show authenticity, ensure your brand's core values. In my experience, consumers tend to prefer brands that they can personally relate to and feel understood. It requires you to be authentic and unique. As a result, you can earn recognition and loyalty from consumers.

5. Always be the better brand.

People give high regard and respect to brands that genuinely help and give back to the community. Promoting campaigns and creating charitable events can improve your image, but most important, your business will be able to help those who need it most. Display a sense of responsibility and commitment to improving the lives of your consumers. Especially during this pandemic, ensure your brand is learning how to step back and create a positive, lasting impact. No matter how big or small the gesture is, this helps tip the scale toward progress and recognition.

Starting a business is never an easy task to handle, and it requires plenty of time and resources to make everything succeed. These strategies are constantly evolving, but the same goal remains: to stay true to the brand's values and offer quality services and products to consumers. Stay updated and learn new tricks of the trade to gain better positions for the business to prosper. May these five pointers provide great insights into creating a successful yet meaningful business that will positively impact your community.

Got A Bad Review?

Don't Take It Personally. Learn from the negative feedback and do not take it too personally. An entrepreneur will evolve by taking this criticism as a framework for growing the company. Go over all the reviews that people post, and don't let anger take over. Most importantly, I apologize for their experience. I believe the most vital element that a brand should obtain from the target audience is trust. Without trust, it's harder to attain an increase in exposure and following. The lack of credibility can eventually lead to failure for the brand to grow and loss of sales. Through video marketing, thought leadership pieces, specialized events, and more, public relations can help bridge the business and the target consumers. Customers tend to gravitate toward relatable brands and encourage their employees to promote the company's brand values, message, and story. It helps small businesses portray a more professional image to current clients and potential customers. To be brand consistent, your employees need to represent the core values no matter their role in the company.

Harness the Power of Storytelling in Three Steps

Everyone loves to listen to a good story. Having the knack to deliver a narrative that fascinates listeners proves to be a good advantage. Storytelling has always captivated my interests. As a founder of a digital marketing agency and a podcast host, I find storytelling a valuable tool that efficiently draws people's attention. It creates more opportunities and connections that promote the growth and recognition of your brand.

The art of storytelling has existed since time immemorial. It can spark inspiration to the masses and create a rippling effect of change and revolution. So, what makes a good story? How do you create stories that not only attract your target audience but also convince them to take action?

Here are three steps to mastering the art of storytelling and harnessing its power in sales.

1. **Grasp the critical elements of a good story.** Anyone can cover a report in various ways, but it

doesn't mean that each is effective and meaningful. There are elements to consider before creating that *big* story that will thrust your brand to phenomenal heights. If you want to use storytelling as your marketing strategy, it is imperative to learn the following elements: the hero, the plot, and the solution.

- The *hero* is the main character. In the marketing scheme, the hero should be your target audience. Involve them in your story. As the protagonists, they immerse themselves into the situation, making it more realistic and relevant.

- The *plot* pertains to the problems they encounter. Use examples that typically happen in daily living and not hypothetical scenarios. The closer the situations are to reality, the easier it is for the audience to visualize the plot.

- The *solution* should be your product or service that uniquely resolves the plot. The hero must see the transformation happen where your brand actively solves the problem.

Every element is vital to forming an inspiring story. Before crafting one, study your target market first and do your research. When you understand your audience more, your goals become more visible and attainable. hoose your plot carefully and make sure that it is realistic and relevant to the present situation. Don't veer off to overly imaginative setups that are hard to believe or too good to be true. Present your solution in the most authentic way possible. Show your audience how your brand offers the best answer without any hype. Remember to keep it straightforward.

2. **Step into the right place at the right time.** Storytelling in sales requires precision and timing. You merely cannot show your cards whenever you wish. Knowing when to tell your story creates a remarkable advantage for your brand.

Here are some examples of the best times to make use of storytelling:

- Introducing your brand to the public: Launching your brand is the perfect time to connect with the audience. It is also your chance to wow them with your story. Demonstrate what your brand is all about and who you are.

- Selling a new product or new service: Introducing a new product or service to the market. Make sure to craft a good story that provides context to clients and makes them visualize how your brand can improve their lives.

- Making use of presentations: Stories incorporated in presentations help entice the audience. After grabbing their attention, reinforce your presentation with facts and simple data that the listeners can understand and easily relate to.

Timing plays a significant role in achieving powerful storytelling. If misplaced, the story could fall flat and be an essential interpreter awkwardly. People may find it overrated if you keep bombarding them with inconsistent or ill-timed narratives out of the blue. Take advantage of creating plans equipped with time frames to ensure that you and your team are on the right track.

3. **Understand the effects and influence of storytelling.** Humans are hard-wired to listen to and

become intrigued by stories regardless of age, gender, and other factors. Throughout human history, storytelling persists in every culture and permeates in each individual. By understanding the effects and responses that storytelling commands, you can successfully use its influence in your favor.

An impressive story arouses curiosity and interest. It triggers the release of specific hormones such as cortisol and oxytocin and stimulates the listeners to connect and empathize with the storyteller. Bear in mind that a good story must have a combination of logic and emotion to incite both sides of the brain. If you only present facts and information alone without igniting feelings, your story will fall short. By infusing human emotions into your stories, people have a greater chance to remember what they felt when they listened to your brand.

With the power of storytelling, leaders can build communities and inspire people to take action. It is also true in sales and marketing. Entrepreneurs can also influence the market with the right strategy of storytelling. It builds relationships, forms trust, and transforms thoughts into actions.

I've used various techniques of storytelling and discovered that it isn't a one-size-fits-all approach. Some strategies work wonders, while others may need improvements. Evolution always takes place. What I do know is – as long as you are passionate and continue to craft new ideas, you will never run out of real stories that captivate and resonate with your audience.

An Expert Tip for Business Negotiations

Learn More About the Other Person

To negotiate effectively, one should learn more about the person they are meeting. It is essential to research the other negotiator to reveal their strengths and weaknesses. One should consider the vendor's or client's needs and the value they add to the business. It's super important to check out the negotiator's website, social pages, or press releases to gather information.

A Final Word

*

How to Master Your Unique Voice as A Business Professional

We all have a voice within us that can be powerful and impactful to others when heard.

So how can we, as business leaders and entrepreneurs, amplify that voice from within us?

I formulated my acronym – **BEPIC** – which helped me overcome moments of weakness to this day.

The art of finding and speaking your unique voice may not be easy, but as long as you're willing to take the first step to greatness, everything else can follow.

Let's Take a Look at What the Experts Have to Say About the Power of BEPIC

Jim Britt: Impactful Top 50 Keynote Speaker

We will get what we have been getting if we do what we have been doing. Get out of your comfort zone. Liana Zavo PR, PRESS AND MEDIA EXPERT-ASK HOW

Lorrie Hargis: Founder of International School of Aromatherapy

In life, it's important to get out of your comfort zone and do things that make you uncomfortable. That might mean taking risks or listening to new ideas even if they don't seem right at first – you may be surprised by how much this helps in developing yourself as a business person Liana Zavo PR, PRESS AND MEDIA EXPERT-ASK HOW

Parthiv Shah, Mr. Implementation: Author of Business Kamasutra

Poor leadership hurts productivity and morale. A strong leadership voice increases your influence and enables you to communicate more effectively with others. Liana Zavo PR, PRESS AND MEDIA EXPERT-ASK HOW

Glenn Bill: America's #1 Attitude Keynote Speaker

You need to have the right attitude if you want to have your own voice...find out what works for you and what doesn't, ask feedback and be open about it. Liana Zavo PR, PRESS AND MEDIA EXPERT-ASK HOW

Tim S. Marshall: Trains Executives & Business Owners to Be Fearless

Opening yourself up to the unknown is more challenging but allows for potential new experiences, skills improvement, and professional and personal growth opportunities. <u>Liana Zavo PR, PRESS AND MEDIA</u> <u>EXPERT-ASK HOW</u>

Rusty Jensen: VP of Revenue Generation

Your professional voice is a key part of your brand. It's what differentiates you from the competition and makes it easier for customers to trust that they're talking with someone who knows their stuff! <u>Liana Zavo PR, PRESS</u> <u>AND MEDIA EXPERT-ASK HOW</u>

About the Author

Liana Zavo, a college drop-out, and a single mom turned millionaire, is on a mission to inspire the world, one woman at a time. Her successful PR agency ZavoMedia Group, based in New York City, helps clients globally secure media opportunities. The woman-run boutique agency, launched in 2017, is now expanding to secure placements for clients in Paris and Dubai. Liana is a Columnist for Forbes and Entrepreneur Magazine and is an official member of Forbes Business Council, Young Entrepreneur Council (YEC), and Chairwoman of WMW Lounge. In addition, she is the chief editor of her business and lifestyle magazine and a celebrated keynote speaker. She is celebrating her accomplishments as the first female entrepreneur and best-selling author in her family.

Growing up, Liana received her first taste of entrepreneurship from her family business. The family owns multiple restaurants and catering halls throughout New York. Even though it would have seemed to be the obvious choice to continue in her family's footsteps and work within the business, Liana had the dreams she needed to chase. She wanted to create a legacy and not take the easy way out and work for her family. So, she started a PR and digital branding boutique agency, ZavoMedia Group, on the strength of her industry experience in branding strategies and public relations with the mindset to give voice to female entrepreneurs. within their journeys and inspire women to become an authority in their niche.

Additionally, Liana developed a platform of podcasts and interviews of executive female mentors who offer successful tips and guidance to women as they embark or continue the entrepreneurship journey. These platforms concentrate on personal branding, content marketing, brand awareness, leading with confidence, authenticity, and how to push through various obstacles of adversity.

When Liana was 15 years old, she didn't have specific goals written down on how she could and would eventually get into television and the mass media industry. Her dream was to be a storyteller and share people's stories with the public. Liana aspired to be on television. Her maternal grandmother was a successful journalist in Russia, traveling the world and covering stories. Her uncle from her paternal family, who is in his late eighties, is the first male author in the Zavo family. She has always been significantly inspired and driven towards her passion from a young age.

As the founder and CEO of ZavoMedia Group and chief editor of *her business and lifestyle magazine*, Liana is responsible for designing successful PR campaigns and brand content to drive brand awareness and for helping leaders navigate complexity with confidence and clarity. With over a decade of experience under her belt, she became a columnist for *Forbes* and *Entrepreneur Magazine, highlighting female-founded startups and championing their success.*

Liana's first primary source of inspiration is her son, Joshua, a sophomore in high school. He launched his businesses JB Mava Corp and Go Tech Doc, a digital marketing agency for solopreneurs, and a cellphone repair boutique shop making him the first young entrepreneur in the family among his fourteen younger cousins. Not only does Liana want to provide choices and opportunities for him that she did not have when she was young, but she wants to show her son that anybody can make a difference in the world. Anything is possible with hard work and dedication.

Liana's second source of inspiration is providing a successful example to other women and proving that they can make their dreams a reality if they stay focused on the goal. She believes we all have a voice within us that can be powerful and impactful to others when heard. For some, it is life-changing. Speaking up endows more self-confidence and brings in newfound peace and growth. Being in the media industry for over a decade, Liana witnessed and went through different scenarios that tested her voice as a PR strategist, speaker, and media mogul. She admits that it wasn't an easy journey, but she didn't end up empty-handed by learning from her experience and extracting the moral lessons.

There were situations when Liana felt unheard, powerless, and limited by her surroundings. However, in those struggles, she pushed herself and broke through her limits, and from then on, she didn't allow anyone to trample on who she is and what she is capable of doing. Fueled with the desire to succeed, she decided to step forward and start speaking up for herself rather than staying in the shadows, and her goal is to inspire others to do the same.

About the Book

The next generation of aspiring professionals is the future of American business. The evidence is everywhere that women today need to have that authority to empower them.

The steps to becoming an authority and expert might not look the same for everyone, but we need to be the new voices of this great new age. This powerful self-help book combines steps to harness your story that will encourage you to break free from your limiting beliefs to speak up, use your powerful voice, be seen, be heard, and become an authority.

Throughout Liana Zavo's early adult years, she felt voiceless and unheard. It made her realize that there is so much to live for than staying invisible. After breaking free from the shackles of silence, she found her way to becoming unforgettable in the mass media industry and breaking the glass ceiling as an immigrant from Russia.

"Effective personal branding is crucial in today's day and age. It will differentiate you from the competition and allow you to build trust with potential clients. You only get one chance to make the best first impression, and that should not be taken lightly."

-Liana Zavo

Liana is to help you see that your voice matters. Every woman can become an expert in her niche, create a signature style, and have a life filled with confidence, visibility, credibility, and the use of an authoritative voice. She is on a mission to help one million women like you gain the courage and confidence to turn that inner voice into a powerful voice and develop authority and become empowered. In this powerful book, there are steps and gathered resources that you can use to improve yourself—the *5 Simple Hacks to BEPIC.*

You, too, can **BEPIC**, an authority, expert, and a powerhouse in your life!